The Legend Of The
Rat King

Norman Nawrocki

Also by Norman Nawrocki

Agitate! Anarchist rants, raps, poems
No Masters! No Gods! Dare to dream
Cazzarola! Anarchy, Romani, Love, Italy
Red: Quebec student strike and social revolt poems
Nightcap for Nihilists
Dinner for Dissidents
Lunch for Insurgents
Breakfast for Anarchists
The Anarchist & The Devil Do Cabaret
Chasseur de Tornades
Rebel Moon: @narchist rants & poems
Resist Much – Obey Little
Rhythm Activism Live

The Legend Of The
Rat King

Norman Nawrocki

Illustrated by

Ivan Radenkovic

LES PAGES NOIRES
MONTREAL

THE LEGEND OF THE RAT KING

Published in 2016 by Les Pages Noires, Montreal, Quebec, Canada
LPN031B

rhythm@nothingness.org
www.nothingness.org/music/rhythm

'A Buck A Body,' and **'The Rat King,'** were first published in 'Rebel Moon: @narchist Rants & Poems' (AK Press, Oakland, 1997), by Norman Nawrocki;
'Rat King,' the song/poem, was originally recorded & released in Montreal by Rhythm Activism on the band's 'Louis Riel in China' cassette (Les Pages Noires, 1988). The album was first launched on Polish National Radio in Warsaw;
'500 Years of Waiting,' the song/poem, was originally recorded & released in Montreal by Rhythm Activism on the band's 'Tumbleweed' cassette (Les Pages Noires, 1993). The piece was dedicated to the non-profit community Mohawk radio station CKHQ 101.7fm, at Kanahsatake, north of Montreal.

Printed and bound in Canada by Gauvin on recycled, acid-free paper

ISBN 978-2-9805763-8-6
Canadian Cataloguing in Publication Data:
Nawrocki, Norman
THE LEGEND OF THE RAT KING

Dépot légal - Bibliothèque et Archives nationales du Québec, 2016
Dépot légal - Library and Archives Canada, 2016

Cover art, all illustrations: Ivan Radenkovic
Book design and production: Mathieu Chartrand

Distributed in Canada by Les Pages Noires Distribution
Distributed in USA & Europe by AK Press www.akpress.org

CONTENTS

AUTHOR'S NOTE

The Legend of the Rat King was originally conceived as an urban gothic rock opera by our 'cabaret rock 'n roll band,' Rhythm Activism (RA). I wrote the words. We performed the show only once, October 15, 1990, at the former Bar La Terrace on Mount Royal in Montreal, Quebec, Canada.

For that show, RA was Sylvain Côté (baritone guitar, vocals), Elaine Stef (drums), and myself (violin, vocals).

The original music composed by Sylvain Côté was quite dramatic to compliment the tone of my texts and noteworthy for it's use of non-traditional time signatures of 5/4 and 11/4.

We had announced a **Rat King** cassette album launch for December 1990, but neither recorded nor released it. We had also planned to expand and tour the show the following year but didn't secure funding for it. The portrait photos of inner-city residents in this book were for that show. Finally, we intended to publish a **Rat King** colouring book, but that too, was shelved. Instead, we pursued other new RA musical and theatrical projects. This book chronicles one of many creative moments in the long and celebrated history of Rhythm Activism.

I thank my talented colleagues in RA, Sylvain Côté and Elaine Stef, for their work in realizing the original magical musical/theatrical project; Ivan Radenkovic for his wonderful artistic collaboration that allows us to delve further into the spirit and imaginary world of the **Rat King**; and Mathieu Chartrand for bringing the text and artwork together with his meticulous and masterful eye.

I dedicate this book to all the Rat Kings and Queens everywhere, past, present and to come.

– Norman Nawrocki
Montreal, Quebec

0

Synopsis

"The Law, in its majestic equality, forbids the Rich as well as the Poor to sleep under bridges, to beg in the streets and to steal bread."

– Anatole France

HE TRIED and didn't succeed,
so he robbed and killed for a dollar.
And he was tried and they succeeded,
so they branded him a criminal,
took his life, and left him a memory.

WHEN the Angels of Death
escorted him to meet the Devil below,
he shook with anger
and was reminded of all his prayers
to a hollow, uncaring God who never answered.
He knew he stood condemned and damned,
but when he refused to submit,
he was sent back – to Hell on earth.
As he started to climb,
he heard the wailing of others
and the clanging of their cages
plunging into the darkness around him.
But he couldn't stop, he couldn't help,
so he kept on climbing.

HANDS TORN and bleeding, he reached the top
and crawled out exhausted and blind
into the noisiest intersection
of the past and the present,
into the heat of the City.
On hands and knees he wove his way
past honking cars and trucks,
through broken bottles, garbage and dog shit,
unable to see, unable to shed a tear,
until he found himself in a bar.
He listened to a story of the First People,
a story of determination.
And he was confused.
When he was heaved out the door,
he stumbled into the gutter and tried to weep,
but he couldn't.

AS HE sat there trying to make sense of the world,
a 14 year old boy, already hundreds of tricks old,
put an arm around his shoulder
and helped him to his feet.
The boy took him home, nursed him, fed him,
cradled him in his arms and told him a story,
a story of courage.
And he was confused.

HE LAY there
in the shell of a rusted, stinking garbage truck
on a mattress stained with blood and beer.
Outside he heard sirens screaming,
gun shots ringing,
and babies crying at their mothers' breasts.
He heard police clubs
beating the flesh of the innocent.
And high above a City dry as tinder,
he heard neon lights exploding into stars of wonder.
He saw the past, he saw tomorrow,
and he saw himself lost somewhere in between.
He cried.
As storm clouds gathered to swell raging sewers,
he knew he was not alone.
He knew what to do.

WHEN he died, the youth cried and buried him
in the dump under the garbage.
Gulls circled overhead and called to each other:
"Son of a broken moon
Born on the third floor of the Sunrise
Abandoned in the alley
Rescued by the rain"
Weeds and stray cats spoke of him lovingly.

SOON it was the Summer of Discontent.
Desire burned holes into the melting pavement.
The Rat King slipped into the darkness,
smiling.

1

A**ND** the Angels of Death
visited prisoner Robert S,
condemned to die,
because he robbed
and he killed
for a dollar,
Oh my!

"So you ran out of luck buddy
chasing a lousy buck
If you'd prayed to us sooner,
we could have tipped you off to a winner,
because

A buck a body is no way to get rich
But dig a hole deep enough
and you'll bury that itch

"Let's say you could have prayed for a factory
to mass produce misery,
maiming and polluting at will,
your own license to kill
We could have blessed your enterprise
showered you with Holy Water,
made you rich and famous
a proud father with sons and daughter
You could have stood tall in the community
Mr Respectable, given to charity
and if anyone noticed the crimes of your factory
shrugged it off with a business morality,
because

A buck a body is no way to get rich
But dig a hole deep enough
and you'll bury that itch"

And the Angels of Death
looked prisoner Robert S straight in the eye
and sighed

"What a pity, why?
You know you could have prayed
for a seat in government
been courted by hawks for peace
voted to outfit killer armies
to protect the pure
and slaughter the diseased
No one would question the connection,
ask the amount of your cut
You'd be defending 'Freedom'
and the right to make your buck,
because

A buck a body is no way to get rich
But dig a hole deep enough
and you'll bury that itch

You could have lobbied with whiskey
to make the death penalty the law
for any poor sucker
who tried to do it his own way
Then on the day the news broke,
about a dollar heist, a dollar stiff,
we'd have propped you up, frothing and blue
to denounce the crime
and the shocking motive, too
Instead you poor bugger,
it's You who's going to die
A needle up the arm, no one will cry,
because

A buck a body is no way to get rich
But dig a hole deep enough
and you'll bury that itch"

And prisoner Robert S
listened to the Angels of Death
and shaking his head, twitching after the injection,
muttered under his last breath:

"A buck a body, it's no way to get rich
So dig me a hole deep enough
and bury me beside someone already rich
I want to borrow their suit
and come back dressed to kill
Then I can gouge the innocent,
gouge the poor
and pay your bill"

And the Angels of Death left prisoner Robert S
alone to die
because he robbed
and he killed
for a dollar,
Oh my!

2

The Descent

AND the Angels of Death
took prisoner Robert S
swiftly down below
where deep among tunnels,
amid a stench and fires burning
the Devil stood waiting to claim his poor soul
As soon as Robert saw the Devil,
he let out a blood-curdling 'NO!'

"I lived my life as honest poor men do
and where did it get me?
Nowhere, but into the gutter
and behind bars, too
I fought back as anyone else would
You've no right to me now, is that understood?"

The Devil sighed,
rolled his eyes,
cleared this throat
then threw the dice:

“One, you’re a liar
Six times a cheat
Ten deadly temptations
Seven days a week
Four times caught
Two years ago
Three different stories
for everyone you know”

But Robert stood unmoved on coals burning
and in the glow of the hellish inferno
recalled all the years of pleading and yearning:

“I prayed for help, no one would listen
I begged out loud, my pleas always forbidden
How many doors slammed in my face?
Each one an echo of my disgrace”

Again, the Devil sighed,
rolled his eyes,
cleared his throat
and threw the dice:

"Eight men swore
Nine times you robbed
Twelve poorer than you
Eleven years counting
Ten times you wanted to die
Five thought suicide
You cursed the Lord
You survived on pride
You refused to obey
To submit as others do
You knew the rules, mister
You broke them all, too"

And Robert, now shaking,
fists clenching in disbelief
cursed the Devil
and smashed him in the teeth:

"Screw your scorecard, your loaded dice
Screw your injustice, your demands for sacrifice
My Hell was to survive everyday
Nights I couldn't sleep, gnawing on my dreams
tormented by no escape
If I wronged others, the choice wasn't mine
I was backed against a wall of misery and despair
I was forced to cross the line"

And the Devil scowling,
spat out a tooth bloody and broken,
and pointing above said:

"Then go back to your own Hell
asshole, back to the living dead!"

3

The Ascent

AND the Angels of Death
led prisoner Robert S,
condemned again and again,
to a swaying chain
that dropped from above
and ordered him to ascend

As he started to climb the dangling line
below him opened a fiery abyss
spewing leaping flames,
hot and merciless

His eyes bulged with fear,
his hands struggling to reach higher
His skin singed and burned started to shred
while all around him,
through the billowing smoke and ash
he saw and heard the rattle and clank of cages
as they descended
filled with the nameless, the faceless,
the shrieking dead

Prostitutes, addicts, panhandlers,
homeless, the sick and hungry
Drifters, the luckless like him,
those without money
All begging for someone
to have mercy on their souls:
"We did nothing wrong!"
"Doesn't anyone know!"

And he closed his eyes and tried not to pray
And tried not to hear
the condemned on their way
He kept on climbing while all around him
the cages kept descending
filled with the forgotten, the forsaken,
the howling dead

He climbed for an eternity
until far above he could see
five points of light clearly
When he reached the top gasping for air,
he pushed aside the red hot steel cover
and found himself back – in the noisiest,
dirtiest, hottest intersection of the City
As he crawled out on hands and knees
he rubbed his eyes in complete surprise
and screamed –
because he couldn't see

On hands and knees,
stumbling, groping,
lost and confused
he couldn't see,
cars and trucks honking,
racing by
But he couldn't see,
and he couldn't cry,
On hands and knees
this half-burned, half-naked,
sewer refugee

4

500 Years of Waiting

YOU know the kind of bar:
table top soaked in beer
puke-stained floor
glistening with excess cheer
a bored stripper in the corner
dancing for the mirror
And louder than her music,
dozens of loaded voices
cannon-balled into smoke so thick,
wild shots aiming for someone's ear,
that special someone nowhere near

But as I staggered blindly
through the tavern door
a First Nations man watched me
weaving across the floor
and grabbing my arm he said:
  "What's the matter white man, can't you see?
   Then sit down friend, I've been waiting for you
   Maybe you'll listen, maybe you'll see
   The others won't – but then, that's my history"

As I listened, he took a swig of beer
raised his glass to the air
and told me his story

He called the forests and I swear,
the pine trees whistled
He called the caribou,
they tossed their heads and ran
He called the eagles,
they spread their wings and soared
He called the fish,
they leaped the falls so high, I could see it all!
Then he started to growl,
He started to roar
His was a voice
I'd never heard before

"500 years of waiting!
500 years of waiting!
500 years of waiting!
And now our time has come!"
(refrain)

"Oh Mother how you've suffered
Oh Mother how you've cried
We tried to stop their wheels turning
how hard we tried
We tried to stop their blades whirling
that cold sharp steel
But their Generals chained our wrists,
forced us to kneel"

And he started to growl,
He started to roar,
His was a voice
I'd never heard before

"They drove us from our homes, you know
and stole our sacred lands
They bled our rivers dry
and banned our sacred dance
When all was said and done
they blamed us for our woes
Well now the circle's closed
So sling the arrows, string the bows!"

And he started to growl,
He started to roar,
He spoke with a voice
I'd never heard before
like a wounded, raging bear

He called the Sun
and the fireball glowed brighter
He called the winds,
they brought clouds and thunder
He called the mountains,
the rocks started rolling
He called the rivers
and they burst the dams asunder
I could see it all!
And he stood on his feet
and smashed the glass
and he started to growl,
he started to roar
He was a wounded, raging bear

5

Johnny

JOHNNY found the blind man
sitting on a curb
He would have been easy to roll
in the empty street
but Johnny already had
a pocket full
of a crumpled bill
and he just wanted someone
to talk to
He'd come out of the salt mines
and just wanted
someone to talk to

Johnny was only 14
but already hundreds of tricks old
He put his arm around
the blind man's shoulders
and invited him home
"Nothing fancy," he said,
"An abandoned garbage truck
near the City Dump"
He'd had worse
at least no one bothered him,
no roaches, no rent
and it was close to work,
where kids go when they're broke
to the salt mines

Johnny sat the blind man down
on an old mattress
a candle threw dancing shadows
up the rusty steel walls
The blind man didn't say much
as Johnny rattled on
about how he ran away from home
because his father would beat him,
suck him off,
throw him against a wall if he cried
How he'd traded a bit of head
for some food and a bed
How he'd ask for 25 bucks,
the men would offer ten,
but he would have settled for five
in the salt mines

Where respectable men go
the teachers, lawyers, doctors,
judges and preachers all
to the salt mines

Johnny knew where to find
the unpicked up orders
of old burgers and pizza
in dumpsters,
but tonight, as he fondled
the crumpled bill in his pocket
he gave the blind man
his only blanket
and said he'd be back
with two hot dogs, cokes,
and a box of donuts
  "You know, a guy needs a buddy
    around here to survive," he said
down by the salt mines
where love goes
when it's lost its soul,
to the salt mines

6

I Hear

I hear the well-fed righteous
  preach about sin
I hear the apostles of the Right
  blame the poor again
I hear hungry babies crying
  at their mothers' breasts
I hear champagne flowing
  into the gutter at the Ritz

I hear fire alarms ringing
I hear bullets singing
I feel the heat approaching
I hear the old world burning
 (refrain)

I hear jackhammers turning
  towers of darkness into dust
I hear channel selectors choosing
  to self-destruct
I hear howling winds ripping
  the glitter off corporate skins
I hear battering rams grunting:
  "Now everyone wins'"

I hear the credit-cardless forgetting
  how to stretch a dime
I hear canned TV laughter
  running out of time
I hear boutique windows shatter
  another mannequin runs
I hear armies of the homeless
  grabbing guns

7

Rat King

SON of a broken moon
Born on the third floor of the Sunrise
Abandoned in the garbage
Rescued by the rain
The beloved Rat King

The Rat King lives in the bus shelter
at the corner of Hastings and Main
and shits in the bank
The Rat King rips open doors
to the City Jail to let the sunshine in
and the prisoners out
The Rat King blows fresh sea air
into musty rooms
where light bulbs swing
and hot plates glow
The Rat King snares bullets
in his bare hands
and smokes them
on the courthouse steps

Raised in the shadow
of the scrawny green door
Wizened by the curve of a sucker punch
Smoother than the Mayor's shave
Smarter than a baseball bat
The beloved Rat King

The Rat King brings pizza all-dressed
with juicy roaches to the stately homes
of hotel slumlords
The Rat King bowls with the balls
of uptown Johns
who jerk off without paying
then tells their wives
The Rat King takes politicians
by their tongues
and whirls them over his head
into the City Dump
The Rat King sends gulls
to lonely window sills
where old timers sit and wait

Denounced by the Pope
Blessed by a one-eyed crow
Blinded by the glare
from a Cadillac's hubcap
Nursed in the palm
of a Japanese cherry blossom
The beloved Rat King

The Rat King ladles extra gravy
onto the mashed potatoes
when the cook isn't looking
The Rat King makes the knives all silent
when they squabble and turn within
The Rat King gives an arm to the feeble,
a voice to the timid
a kick to those stuck in the muck
The Rat King walks barefoot
on butts burning
and lets his people
through the turnstiles – no charge
At night, the Rat King
rests his head on a bench
and talks to the gods

Son of a broken moon
Born on the third floor of the Sunrise
Memorized by alley cats and weeds
Dead for a thousand years
The beloved Rat King

A series of photos the author took in Vancouver's inner-city Downtown Eastside, January, 1991, with the consent of each person. The photos were to be used for an expanded live performance and tour of the show. The names have been changed here.

Alec, on East Pender. He said he was one of the lucky ones with an affordable, clean room. "The roaches don't bother me as much as the addicts did at my other place."

Steve, in an alley off Hastings Street. Retired from the army, walks with a cane. Got robbed of $800 recently. Called it his "initiation into Vancouver," the big city.

Frank Joe, outside the San Francisco Pawnbrokers. A poet and musician, clean for one month, no drugs, no alcohol, just cigarettes. Has a writing table in his room. Will be published in the next Carnegie Community Centre Newsletter.

Andrew, sitting on a bench in Victory Square. Wondered why would anyone want to take his picture when there were so many pretty girls around?

John, on Powell Street. Moved down from Terrace, BC, but finds it too expensive here to live on his meagre pension. Was having a by-pass operation. Said that maybe he doesn't want a successful one, that maybe death would be better.

Eddy, on Powell. Used to be in show business. Wore huge rings on all his fingers. Said he once was a real big shot, had keys to Cadillacs. Now, uses a motorized wheel chair and needs help to enter the bars.

Mike, in an alley off Main Street. From the Saulteaux First Nation, from Regina. Going to see his girlfriend who works at the carwash on Hastings Street.

Leszek, on Powell Street. He left Hungary in 1956 after the revolt. Got hit by a car twice in a nearby intersection. Hates all cops. Said that the heroin dealers were buying off the cops.

Jacques, on Columbia Street. Moved here from Quebec 14 years ago. Was sick of digging tiles. Now washes windows at the Sunrise Hotel.

Norman Nawrocki

Discography

Rhythm Activism

Biography

Ivan Radenkovic

Biography

Norman Nawrocki Discography

Solo & with his different bands
(See Les Pages Noires catalogue online for available recordings)

HEAVENLY DEVILS, DaZoque! – CD, 2016, Les Pages Noires, Montreal
WILD PLAINS: LIVE IMPROVISATIONS – CD, 2015, LPN, Mtl
YOMA, Original Motion Picture Soundtrack, CROCODILE – CD, 2015, Crocorecordz, Mtl
CROCODILE LIVE A QUEBEC CITY – cass, 2014, Crocorecordz, Mtl
CAZZAROLA! Anarchy, Romani, Love, Italy – CD, 2013, LPN, Mtl
LETTERS FROM POLAND / LETTRES DE POLOGNE – CD, 2006, LPN, Mtl
SANN – CD, 2005, LPN, Mtl.
DUCK WORK – CD, 2004, LPN, Mtl.
THE MONTREAL MANHATTAN PROJECT – CD, 2004, LPN, Mtl.
DAZOQUE! – CD, 2002, LPN, Mtl.
FIGHT TO WIN! – CD, 2001,
G7 Welcoming Committee Records, Winnipeg
I DON'T UNDERSTAND WOMEN! – cass, 1993, LPN, Mtl.
OVERDALE RAG – cass, 1987, Jelly Bean, Montreal, Mtl.

With my band Rhythm Activism:

JESUS WAS GAY – CD, 1998,
G7 Welcoming Committee Records, Winnipeg
BUFFALO, BURGERS & BEER – cass, 1995, LPN, Mtl.
MORE KICK! – CD, 1995, LPN, Mtl. / Konkurrel, Amsterdam
BLOOD & MUD – CD, 1994, LPN, Mtl. / Konkurrel, Amsterdam / Cass, 1997, Nikt Nic Nie Wie, Warsaw, Poland
TUMBLEWEED – cass, 1993, LPN, Mtl.
OKA II – cass, 1992, LPN, Mtl.
WAR IS THE HEALTH OF THE STATE – cass, 1991, LPN, Mtl.
OKA - cass, 1990, LPN, Mtl.
PEROGIES, PASTA & LIBERTY – cass, 1990, LPN, Mtl.
FIGHT THE HIKE! – cass, 1990, LPN, Mtl.
UN LOGEMENT POUR UNE CHANSON – cass, 1990, LPN, Mtl.
LOUIS RIEL IN CHINA – cass, 1988, LPN, Mtl.
RESIST MUCH – OBEY LITTLE – cass, 1987, LPN, Mtl.
RHYTHM ACTIVISM "LIVE" – cass,1987, LPN, Mtl.
RHYTHM ACTIVISM – cass, 1986, LPN, Mtl.

COMPILATIONS (SOLO & WITH ALL HIS BANDS):

DUETS FOR ABDELRAZIK – CD, 2012, Howl! Arts Collective, Montreal
ART, ANARCHYf AND ACTIVISM – CD, 2007,
CBC Radio, Toronto
TAKE PENACILIN NOW – CD, 2005,
G7 Welcoming Committee Records, Winnipeg
SPOKEN BROKEN - CD, 2004, Wired on Words, Mtl.
2 TONGUE 5 - CD, 2004, Loose Discs, Quebec
ANARCHIST BLACK CROSS - CD, 2003,
ABC Records, Sao Paolo Brazil
LOVE & RAGE VOL 1 - CD, 2003,
Love & Rage Records, North Richmond, Australia
2TONGUE 4 - CD, 2003, Loose Discs, Quebec
BEYOND 'MAN' HOOD, cass, 2001,
Montreal Men Against Sexism Prod, Montréal
RETURN OF THE READ MENACE - CD, 1999,
G7 Welcoming Committee Records, Winnipeg
PASAZEER - CD, 1999, Pasazer Records, Warsaw, Poland
FOLKOPHOBIA - CD, 1998, Tranzophobia, Chambery, France
LES MYSTERES DES VOIX VULGAIRES #3 - cass, 1997,
Art as Hammer Records, Milano, Italy
LES MYSTERES DES VOIX VULGAIRES #2- CD, 1997,
Art as Hammer Records, Milano, Italy
LESS ROCK MORE TALK - CD, 1997,
AK Press, San Francisco/Edinburgh
KESKIDEEZ - EP, 1997, Broken Ear, California
UP TO D.A.T. - CD, 1997,
Mad's Collectif, Saint-Etienne, France
KING KONK 2 - CD, 1996, Konkurrel, Amsterdam
ZOOCOMPILATION - CD,/cass, 1996,
Trottel Records, Budapest, Hungary
UNIRACIAL SUBVERSION - CD, 1995,
Blackbird Records, Hong Kong
CRISES - CD, 1994, Broken Tapes, Limesay, France
MAIS OU EST PASSE L'ANARCHIE? - cass, 1994,
Broken Tapes, Limesay, France
POGO AVEC LES LOUPS - CD, 1992, On a Faim!, Paris
BITTERSWEET CANADA - CD,/cass, 1992,
Word of Mouth Records, Toronto
ZWOLNA TAPES VOL 1 - cass, 1992,
Zwolna T & R, Metz, France
NIGHTMARE ON ALBION STREET - LP, 1992,
1 in 12 Records, Bradford, England
BRAIN BATTERY - cass, 1991,
Broken Tapes, Limesay, France
JUST LISTEN - cass, 1991, All Genre, Waltham, MA
LES MYSTERES DES VOIX VULGAIRES - CD, LP, cass, 1990, Divergo, Milano, Italy
SUR LA GUERRE DES SEXES (ABOUT SEX WAR) - LP, 1990, P.A.I., Paris
THEFT OF PARADISE - cass, 1988,
Technawabe Sounds, Ottawa
CIA TAPES - cass, 1988, Blurg Records, Bradford, UK
VOICE OF AMERICANISM - cass, 1988, Bad Newz, New York
EXPO HURTS EVERYONE - 7", 1986,
Sudden Death Records, Vancouver

Rhythm Activism Biography

RHYTHM ACTIVISM (RA) was an internationally acclaimed, Montreal-based, 'rock 'n roll cabaret' ensemble co-founded by Norman and Sylvain in 1985. From a simple poetry/music duo, the performance unit evolved into a surprise-packed 'rebel news orchestra' and 'giant musical cartoon.' Versatility was their trademark. They charted on radio worldwide, performed highly memorable theatrical musical shows, and toured their issue-oriented 'resistance cabarets' across Canada, the USA and Europe to rave reviews. The European press called them "the real avant-garde." They performed a riotous brand of independent, theatrical music and song in English, French, Italian and Polish. They appeared on stage as a duo, a four to seven piece band, or with a supporting cast of 50 dancers, jugglers, other musicians, acrobats, clowns and actors in a series of madcap, Felliniesque, anti-poverty 'community circus cabarets.'

PHOTO: Rhythm Activism in 1990, L to R: Elaine Stef, Sylvain Côté, and Norman Nawrocki

RA played theatres, punk clubs, poetry festivals, international jazz and folk festivals, on the barricades at demonstrations, or at traditional Ukrainian weddings, performing a cutting-edge hybrid of folk punk, country and eastern, urban rat jazz, lounge core and infectious East European dance tunes. Always ahead of the news, RA was known as a topical and provocative band whose shows made national and international news. Satirical and hard-hitting, they took on issues of the day using costumes, masks and vaudeville to turn serious politics into subversive but hilarious living theatre.

Critics hailed their work as "powerful," "stunning," and "brilliant," and compared them alternately to Chumbawumba, Tom Waits with a butcher knife, The EX, Fugazi, and even Brecht and Weill. Their informative and rib-tickling political community cabarets – produced jointly with hundreds of tenants and welfare rights groups across Quebec – entertained thousands of the poorest of the poor who packed church basements and soup kitchens for shows.

Their repertoire of 'news poems,' instrumentals and songs numbers over 1000 original pieces. RA's discography: 15 albums plus 25 compilations. RA also has two documentary films and appear on numerous soundtracks. After their 1998 'Jesus Was Gay' world tour, they stopped performing reuniting for two shows only in 2007.

See more: www.nothingness.org/music/rhythm

Ivan Radenkovic Biography

Ivan Radenkovic (aka Ivan Ludi Biciklista) is a painter, illustrator, and tattoo artist based in Belgrade and Montreal. His work spans a range from dark expressionism and painterly montage to pop illustration. He often mines the fantastic, bizarre, dark and playful aspects of childhood, animal spirits, uncanny characters, monsters and unclassifiable creatures with a deep sense of enchantment, oddity, outsiderness, and pathos. He studied at the Academy of Fine Arts at the University of Belgrade with a specialization in painting. He has shown work in both solo and group exhibitions like the Osaka Art Fair, Ljutic, Dom Omladine (Belgrade), Gallery Ili Ili (Belgrade) and the Gallery Krug. He's illustrated children's books and created album art for bands like Di Nigunim and The Thief's Lineage (Blood-Stained Cuffs). A lot of people in Belgrade and beyond wear his tattoos.

Ivan's inspiration:
"to observe and to inhale everyday situations. fascinated with people's abilities to change shape and the emotions that take over and become something physical, leaving a story. seeking for primal attributes and often stepping into that other sphere of innocence and purity of nature. walking between two worlds, of good and bad monsters."

www.paperghosts.org

LES PAGES NOIRES

LES PAGES NOIRES (LPN) is a non-profit, volunteer-run, multi-media publishing, recording, production and distribution project based in Montreal, Quebec, Canada. The project is dedicated to helping create and disseminate dissident, freedom-loving, anarchist-inspired culture that promotes social justice.

FRIENDS OF LPN: LPN operates on the margins with obvious financial constraints that limit the number and frequency of our artistic creations. We welcome outside financial contributions from those who want to support our work. If you'd like to help us:

rhythm@nothingness.org

MORE FROM LES PAGES NOIRES DISTRIBUTION, MONTREAL

BOOKS

AGITATE! Anarchist rants, raps, poems,
by Norman Nawrocki, 80 pages

More incendiary poetics, raps, songs, tall tales, exhortations, dreams and delusions. Out of control police, how to resist war, Kurdish women warriors, Louis Riel, slave revolts and more. Beautifully illustrated by Mathieu Chartrand.

'Nawrocki's life and career would require a shelf full of books to document.'
- Canadian Review of Literature in Performance

No Masters! No Gods! Dare to dream
by Norman Nawrocki, 76 pages, illustrated

Another daring and delightful collection of urban tall tales, fiction, poems, dreams and rhymes for 21st century rebels. Classic texts like, The Velorution, A Wobbly dinner, Montreal! You've got no heart, no art. Wonderfully illustrated by Philtre.

'Every city should be so lucky to have a Norman Nawrocki'
- The Montreal Mirror

CAZZAROLA! Anarchy, Romani, Love, Italy
by Norman Nawrocki, 318 pages

His internationally acclaimed, gripping first novel about 130 years in the life of an Italian family, (anti-fascists) and the romantic story of a Roma refugee woman and her Italian lover.

'I have never read a more delicate portrayal of a Romani woman in my life. Her strength, resilience and brilliance shine. She makes me proud of who I am....'
- Qristina Zavacková Cummings, T'aven Baxtale

'Recognizable characters, believable situations, and a kick ass, gritty love story absent of empty clichés'
- MaximumRockNRoll

'Deftly weaves together characters, time periods, fact, and fiction to create a tapestry that's one-part romance, one-part anti-fascist polemic, and one-part paean to the bravery of anarchists...a great read'
- The Other Press

Déjeuner pour anarchistes, poésie

by Norman Nawrocki, 104 pages, illustrated

The French translation of Nawrocki's best-selling, Breakfast for Anarchists.

'An important figure on the international alternative circuit'
- Ici, Montreal

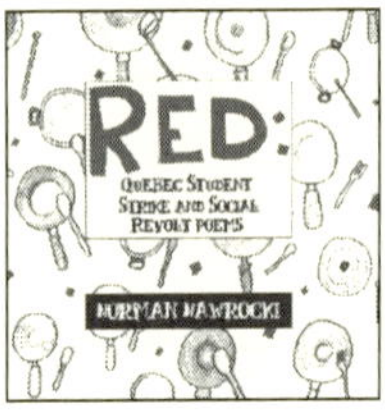

RED: Quebec Student Strike and Social Revolt Poems

by Norman Nawrocki, 104 pages, illustrated

Beautifully bound and illustrated book of his stirring poems documenting the largest ever civil disobedience movement in Canadian history: the 2012 Quebec post-secondary 'red square' student strike.

'Nawrocki is a Montreal legend.'
- The Gazette, Montreal

Nightcap for Nihilists

by Norman Nawrocki, 80 pages, illustrated

Continues Nawrocki's obsession with hammering away poetically at a rotting social order and replacing it with a newly liberated, more just world. Both a battle-cry and an anarchist vision of what's wrong and what to do.

'His delving diatribes pack a punch'
- The Ottawa Xpress

Dinner for Dissidents

by Norman Nawrocki, 80 pages, illustrated

A powerful, rabble-rousing dose of poetic creativity for anyone craving new ways of thinking towards a world without rulers or ruled. Soul-stirring poems, songs and lyrical musings.

'The voice of Nawrocki gives a kick in the head to authoritarian society'
- The Montreal Mirror

Lunch for Insurgents
by Norman Nawrocki, 80 pages, illustrated
More radical poems songs and rants about how thinking imaginative citizens can engage in simple everyday creative resistance.
'One of Canada's most active activist scribes'
– The Vancouver Province

Breakfast for Anarchists
by Norman Nawrocki, 80 pages, illustrated
The first volume in Norman Nawrocki's Brain Food Trilogy. Over 30 provocative, poetic capsules of Nawrocki's trademark wit, passionate rage, love and reflection. Includes his celebrated piece, Why am I an anarchist?
'Highly recommended for the politically astute'
– Broken Pencil

The Anarchist & The Devil Do Cabaret
by Norman Nawrocki, 207 pages
Internationally lauded collection of his short stories, letters and journal entries inspired by a Rhythm Activism band tour of Europe.
'Mirrors the best of cabaret, blending artistry, comedy, and protest into an anthem for social justice.'
– Amazon.ca
'An incredible collection from the untiring anarchist story teller'
– Free Republic

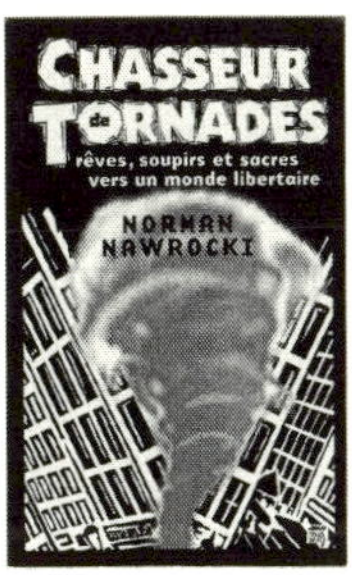

Chasseur de Tornades: Rêves, soupirs et sacres vers un monde libertaire
by Norman Nawrocki, 88 pages, illustrated
Nawrocki's own original and translated poetics, urban legends and rebel songs in French.
'The writing is stamped with Nawrocki's commitment & quest for justice & freedom'
– ICI, Montreal

MUSIC

Heavenly Devils (CD)

by DaZoque!

More cutting-edge instrumental compositions and East European traditional dances, blending acoustic and electric strings with fierce, beat-rich drumming, electric bass, guitar and organ. Neo-classical post-rock and experimental edgy folk. From the two violin centered band (Minda Bernstein & Norman Nawrocki) that wowed critics with their first album.

'Delicious, astonishing, audacious – Le Devoir

'Wedding music for anarchists' – The Globe & Mail

'A luscious soundscape' – The Beat Magazine, Los Angeles

Wild Plains: Live Improvisations (CD)

A stunning and bold 45 minute collection of ten live improvisations from classical pianist Josée Allard & very non-classical violinist Norman Nawrocki. East European flavoured mountain dances, pensive, Irish-inspired midnight explorations, and wild, furious TV cartoon soundtracks. Pieces of startling urgency, beautyand passion.

'Grounded in strong musicianship from different genres... bursting with raw boundless, bold, rhythmic energy.' – Connections, Music for People

Yoma, original motion picture soundtrack (CD)

by Crocodile!

Crocodile is Montreal's exciting post-rock/post stoner/post everything band, with veteran scratch 'n looping heavy wood fiddler Norman Nawrocki, post-punk bassist Philippe Caron, and drummer extraordinaire, Anne-Marie Duclos. Eleven improvised tracks of captivating ambient, instrumental, experimental, non-formulistic and slightly East European music. A soundtrack for a film that was never shot.

CAZZAROLA! The musical soundtrack for the novel (CD)

by Norman Nawrocki & amici (friends)

Sixteen tracks of original and traditional Italian-themed songs (from 1880 today) composed & recorded by Nawrocki and the bands Crocodile, DaZoque!, DisCanto, E Zhivindi & more, in Italy & Canada. Music inspired by or related to his novel, Cazzarola! Anarchy, Romani, Love, Italy (PM Press, 2013). www.cazzarola.ca

'A haunting yet still soothing soundtrack for his novel' – The Gazette, Montreal

Letters from Poland / Lettres de Pologne (CD)

by Norman Nawrocki

Nawrocki plays looped violin, viola, accordion, piano and a 142-string Ukrainian/Polish tsymbaly (hammered dulcimer) and reads 12 letters from The Anarchist & The Devil Do Cabaret sent to his father from a Polish uncle. Poignant, humourous and bittersweet, the letters trace the love and longing of one brother for another and document his growing resistance to Nazism.

'Made me think of the train album that Steve Reich did with regards to the trains taking inmates to Aushwitz....it touched me a lot.' – Radio Canada

Duck Work (CD)

by Norman Nawrocki

A beat-rich, anti-war, anti-Empire onslaught of hypnotic bass, percussive and driving looped violins, viola and cello, with incendiary lyrics and an upbeat call to action.

'A mystic journey through a diverse selection of heavenly looped violins, warm percussion and insightful spoken word. Never a dull moment on the disc.' – Urbnet

DaZoque! (CD)

by DaZoque!

'Urban Montreal meets a Slavic mountain village under a full moon.' Exquisite East European flavoured instrumentals by a string ensemble anchored by the core violin duo of Minda Bernstein and Nawrocki.

'Wedding music for anarchists. While they fiddle, sampled loops & electric guitars burn' – The Globe & Mail

Rhythm Activism, More Kick! (CD)
RA's 14th high-energy release, recorded live in Europe, inspiration for The Anarchist & The Devil.
'Intelligent musical buffoonery' – Bruits, Paris
'Stunning & deeply moving'
– Opscene, Amsterdam

Rhythm Activism, Blood and Mud (CD)
RA's captivating homage to the Zapatista rebellion in Chiapas, Mexico. Nawrocki co-founded RA.
'Brilliant mixture of sound and words'
– Magnet, Philadelphia
'Should be mandatory listening for members of Congress' – Option, L.A.

The Montreal Manhattan Project (CD)
Nawrocki's experimental jazz trio with Aaron Shragge & Greg Anderson Smith. A haunting potpourri of looped cello, viola and violin, with soaring trumpet and sparse, beautiful electronica.

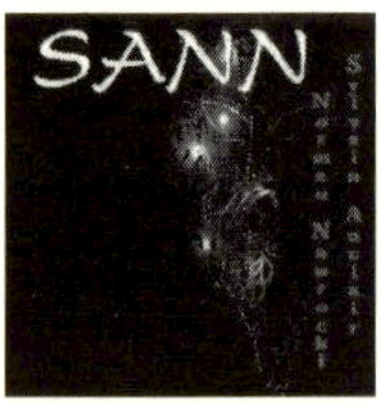

SANN (CD)
Original, atmospheric, ambient creations. Highly imaginary, visual music with Chapman Stick Bass, bass, violin and viola. A duo of Nawrocki and Sylvain Auclair.